Do I Have A Legitimate Auto Accident Claim?

Useful Info That May Help Your Case

Kevin Ginsberg, Esq.

ISBN: 978-1-941645-80-2

Designed and Published by:
Speakeasy Publications
73-03 Bell Blvd, #10
Oakland Gardens, NY 11364
www.SpeakeasyMarketingInc.com
888-225-8594

Disclaimer

This publication is intended to be informational only. No legal advice is being given, and no attorney-client relationship is intended to be created by reading this material. If you are facing legal issues, whether criminal or civil, seek professional legal counsel to get your questions answered.

Taibi Kornbluth Law Group, P.A.
3100 Tower Blvd., Suite 800
Durham, North Carolina, 27707
(919) 328-0508
www.personalinjurydurham.com

TESTIMONIALS

"Thank you for all your help during the past several months, I greatly appreciate the excellent customer service and making my experience memorable with an impeccable victory on October 8th, it was truly such a joy to finally WIN! It has been a pleasure to have worked with you and your group. Again, my sincere gratitude to all."

- Maritis E.

"The attorneys and dedicated staff at Taibi Kornbluth maintain a highly professional, yet relaxed environment. They strive to prepare the best possible case, and keep the client's interests as top priority. They are well aware of the importance of a client's time, and strive to accommodate the client's schedule, not their own."

- Bentley C.

"Thank you so much for all of your help, advice, and time. I have and will continue to pass your name along to others in need of assistance. Have a wonderful Holiday season!"

- S.R.

TABLE OF CONTENTS

AUTHOR INTRODUCTION

I have been licensed to practice law in North Carolina since 2000. During that time I have represented thousands of clients, litigated hundreds of cases, and taken dozens of cases all the way to jury verdicts. In addition to practicing law, I am married since 2002 to Andrea Ginsberg, owner of local gourmet popcorn store, The Mad Popper. We have two wonderful school-age boys. I am also a marathon runner, writer, juggler, semi-professional pickle maker, and totally unprofessional comedian, performing for The Monti and The Murphey School Radio Show.

Education

❖ University of North Carolina School of Law
Doctor of Law (JD), Law

❖ University of North Carolina at Chapel Hill
Bachelor of Science (BS), Business Administration and Management, General

Experience

- Attorney Partner

Taibi Kornbluth Law Group

April 2015 – Present

- Senior Litigation Attorney

Lanier Law Group, P.A.

May 2003 – April 2015

Handle all aspects of personal injury claims, from initial meeting with client to settlement or jury trial.

License

- State: NC
- Status: Active
- Acquired: 2000
- Updated: 10/30/2015

Publications

- Publication name: What Can You Do With A Law Degree? 5th Edition By Deborah Arron
- Title: Alternative Dispute Resolution
- Date: 2003

Steps That You Need To Take After You Are Injured In An Auto Accident

You need to take the following steps as soon as possible after you are injured in an auto accident in North Carolina.

Get Proper Medical Treatment

I don't mean to be crass, but getting injured in a car wreck sucks. Even relatively minor injuries can be nagging, long lasting, and take a toll on your lifestyle. And more serious or catastrophic injuries are obviously that much worse. Regardless, the most important first step to take when you have discovered that you have been injured is that you need to get proper medical treatment. That might mean going to the emergency room, it might mean going to your primary care doctor, it might mean going to an urgent care or to an orthopedist; it really depends on what your injury is. Your health is always the most important thing to take care of immediately.

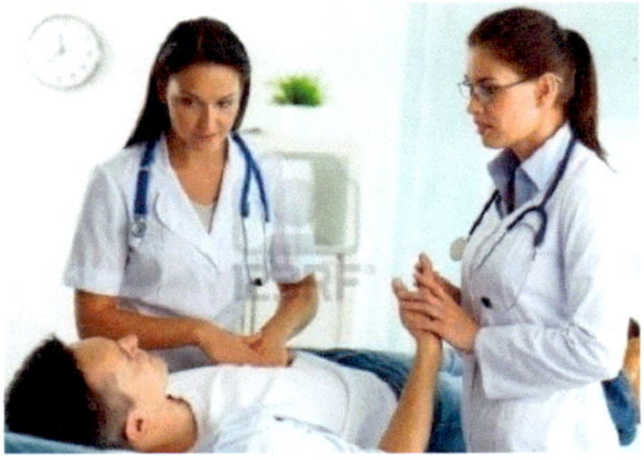

But, (while I might be a biased narrator!) it is also important to at least speak with an attorney as soon as possible so that you know how you can protect your rights. This little booklet can give you some guidance but there will never be a good substitute for actually being able to speak with an attorney about the specifics of you and your case, and actually being represented. You want to find an attorney that you like and that you trust. In some cases you may find that you don't need to hire an attorney, but it can still give you good peace of mind and information to speak with one.

Notify Your Insurance Company

If you don't hire an attorney, you should inform your own insurance company for a number of reasons. Most likely, you have some benefits on your policy that you have paid for through your premiums that you will

want to use. Even if there is an at-fault carrier involved, your own insurance company may have what's called MedPay which is going to be extra money to help pay for medical bills. You should be able to access this money on your own, but an attorney can help you process that for no additional charge.

You might also have what's called underinsured coverage. This can be very important if there is a serious or catastrophic injury and the liability coverage for the at-fault driver is not sufficient to pay for your injuries. Typically, after a car wreck, when a police report is filled out, the other insurance company will be notified. The at-fault driver will notify their own insurance company but they may not and the burden may fall on you to do that. All of this can be taken off of your plate when you hire an attorney; they will send a letter of representation both to your insurance company as well as the at-fault driver's insurance company and everybody will be properly noticed.

You might also need your own insurance company’s help if liability is being investigated by the other carrier. If the at fault carrier delays taking care of the property damage, and you have your own collision, coverage, you can use that in order to speed up the property damage process. Finally, you may need your own insurance company in the unfortunate event that the at-fault is not insured at all; in that case you would need to file an uninsured claim with your own company.

Do Not Give A Recorded Statement To Other Driver's Insurance Company

Adjusters for insurance companies very often will tell you that you are required to make a recorded statement in order to get your property damage taken care of or in order for you to have a claim. That's not the truth. You do not have any legal obligation to give a recorded statement to the insurance company. In some rare circumstances, your attorney may have you give one, but in general you should not be speaking with the adverse insurance company; let your attorney do the talking for you.

Hire An Attorney

OK, this is going to start to sound like a big advertisement for why you should hire an attorney. I guess it kind of is. Again, your attorney will generally deny the insurance company access to a recorded statement. There are exceptions that can be made but, in general, an attorney will not make his clients get a recorded statement with the insurance company.

The attorney can provide them all the information they need without having to have that recorded conversation with you. It's very important for people not to give recorded statements to insurance companies when they are not represented. All kinds of mistakes, particularly costly innocent mistakes, happen when you do that, because you can end up saying things that the insurance company will use against you.

Now it is not uncommon at all that a week or two or even months after a car wreck, someone comes to an attorney for representation after a point in which they have already given a recorded statement to the company. That doesn't mean that your claim is doomed. A good attorney can deal with whatever has happened already but if the attorney is in a position to give advice, he'll tell you not to give a recorded statement to the insurance company.

However, it is a different matter when it comes to your own insurance company. You do have a legal obligation to cooperate with them and give a recorded statement. Therefore, you should have an attorney present during that conversation.

Legal Terms That People Involved In Auto Accidents Must Be Aware Of

There are some legal terms that people involved in auto accidents need to be aware of. Some of them are as following:

Fault And No Fault States

North Carolina is a "fault" state, which requires a showing of fault by someone else for you to be able to be compensated for your injuries. In North Carolina, you need three main facts on your side in order to get compensation for any kind of injury claim including a car wreck claim. You have to show that some other person was at fault for causing a car wreck (that they were negligent), that you were not at fault (that you were not contributorily negligent) and you have to show that you were injured because of the at-fault party's negligence (that there is causation).

Contributory Negligence

North Carolina is one of four states in the country that retains the law of contributory negligence. Contributory negligence is a law that says if you are injured in a car wreck (or in any other potential liability or tort claim) but you were determined to be even partially at fault, then you can't recover anything.

Insurance companies use this law to say that even if their insured was 99% at fault and you were only 1% at fault that you can't recover. That's not exactly what the law says, but that's what the insurance companies will argue. The law just asks if you were injured by the negligence of someone else. There is no percent attached to that and the specific facts are important to determine if there really is fault by the other driver. The law also asks if you, by your own negligence, contributed to your own injury. Again, there is no percentage there and a jury can weigh what that really means. However, insurance companies do often strictly construe that to say if you were at all at fault, even 1%, you can't get anything; this is another reason to have an attorney on your side so that the insurance company doesn't claim you were at fault when you were not.

Attorney Kevin Ginsberg has represented hundreds of people in situations where the insurance company claimed that his client was at fault to some degree and initially denied liability before he got them to change their position, either through a negotiated settlement or through a jury deciding his client was not at fault. That said, if there is a valid factual reason for the insurance company saying that you were partially at fault, that may make successful resolution of your claim more difficult, it might mean that it takes longer, and if you really were at fault then you probably won't be able to recover a settlement. But if you were not at fault, you should still be able to recover a settlement notwithstanding what the insurance company says.

Statute Of Limitations

In North Carolina and throughout the country, most claims that you can bring for any reason have what's called a statute of limitations attached to it. The statute of limitations is a legislated law that dictates that there is a certain timeframe in which you can file a lawsuit to protect your claim.

The law is very strict and very clear in North Carolina about this. You have three years from the date of the incident to file your lawsuit or your claim will be time barred forever. In fact, if you bring a claim with the insurance company, put them on notice in writing; tell them that you have a claim and otherwise make it clear so that they know that you were injured - but you don't file the lawsuit within three years, you will lose. Of course, you can settle your claim before the three-year time period is over and won't ever need to file a lawsuit, but if your claim has not settled, it must be filed as an official lawsuit in the Courts or your claim will be forever time barred.

In North Carolina, the wrongful death statute says that you have two years after a death to file a lawsuit and if the wrongful death was as a result of a car wreck, then that three year period is shortened to two years in which the decedent's estate has to file a lawsuit.

Factors That Play An Important Role In An Auto Accident Case

There are certain factors which play an important role in the timing of damages recovery in an auto accident case. For example:

Time That You Take To Recover From Injuries

The biggest factor for how long it will take for your claim to resolve is how long it takes for your medical symptoms and for your injuries to resolve. The last thing you want to do is settle your case before you have gotten better, or before you really know what the extent of your injuries are. If you have a really bad injury or one that lasts for a long time, you generally at least want to wait until you have reached the 'maximum medical improvement' point before considering settling your case.

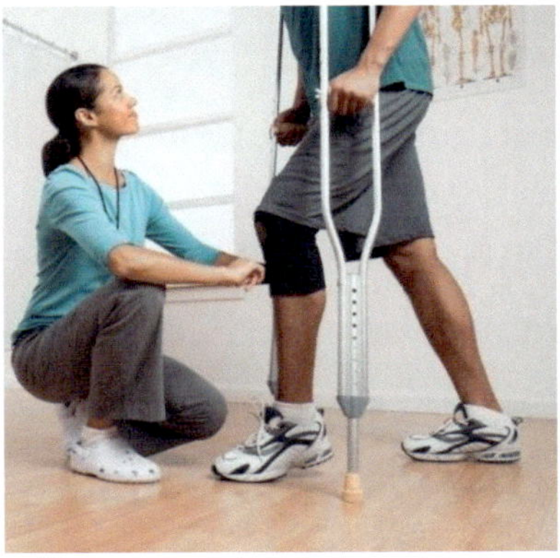

The maximum medical improvement point is where your doctor says you have improved and gotten to a certain point but you may not get any better. They deem you at maximum medical improvement. While you might continue to have symptoms and you may even continue to treat over time, at that point it may be okay to consider a settlement. Again, it's crucial not to settle your case before you're done with your treatment because you really risk selling yourself short. Once there is a settlement, it is going to be final. If you discover that you are hurt worse than you realized, you can't go back and undo that settlement contract.

Once you have finished your treatment or reached maximum medical improvement, whether that takes days, weeks, months or years, then the time that it takes depends on how quickly the attorney is able to access all your medical records and bills and compile them into a demand package to send to the insurance company. That usually takes in the range of weeks or even a few months depending on how extensive your treatment was. Once that has all been sent to the insurance company, the insurance company will take some days or weeks to evaluate and make an offer.

The big and not uncommon exception to all of this is if the claim doesn't get resolved voluntarily - either the insurance company denies and doesn't make an offer or makes too low of an offer – or you and your attorney just decide that filing a lawsuit is in your interest more so than attempting settlement. In those cases, when you file a lawsuit rather than just filing a claim, the timeframe is of course different. That process is time consuming and can take a good year or more to get through an entire litigation process. However, if you have an attorney that you like and trust and he advises you to do that, then it's in your best interest to go that route even if it takes more time. While I represent clients from the very beginning stages of a case all the way through settlement or trial, and while the majority of cases are able to settle without a lawsuit even needing to be initiated, I have represented hundreds of people through the litigation process. We have the experience and infrastructure to go all the way to trial for you if need be.

No Harm, No Foul Rule

If you weren't injured, then you don't have a case that's going to go too far. It's kind of the no harm, no foul rule, although, to be fair, I don't know of any official rule by that name! If someone else rear ends you, they are clearly at fault and you are not contributorily negligent, but if you weren't hurt, then you just want to feel fortunate that you weren't injured. Usually, your property damage will be covered but there is not going to be much of a case beyond that to worry with.

On the other hand, the worse your injury, the more serious you were hurt, the more substantial of a settlement you should expect. There are other factors that go into the size of a case such as if the person who caused the wreck was not only at fault but was also drunk.

That may entitle you to punitive damages. That can, in certain circumstances, substantially increase the amount of money that you are entitled to.

The Size Of The Impact

There are lots of other factors that play a role in your case as well. The size of the impact itself, while it may not seem fair, can and does often change the value of the settlement. This means that if someone gets into a small accident and

has X amount of injury or if someone gets in a large accident and has the exact same X amount of injury, the person in the big wreck with the big property damage is more likely going to get a bigger settlement offer. That's another reason to have an attorney fight for you – because when you are in a smaller impact accident, the insurance company may say that it was too small. You have to make sure that they are not minimizing your claim just because of that.

Importance Of Evidence And Witnesses In Auto Accident Cases

The most important evidence to prove your injury is going to be your medical records and bills from your medical treatment. It's also important to bring in any witnesses or non-medical personnel

to talk about your injuries – in person if in an actual trial, or in writing if through an attempted pre-suit settlement. This could be your friends, family members, coworkers, neighbors, pastor, or other people in your life who knew you before the car wreck and knew you after the car wreck. These people can give credible testimony as to what the impact on your life was and how they view your injuries.

Presenting evidence and witnesses can be done in trial but it can also be done before a lawsuit is even filed to help get a better settlement. Sometimes, car wrecks involve disputed liability or questions of who is at fault. In those cases, it's also crucial to have eye witnesses to the wreck who can testify in your favor as to why it was the other person's fault and not yours.

In some cases, the question of who is at fault is really the question that has to be answered in order to get a fair settlement. In some cases, the question of whether you were injured or how badly you were injured is what has to be answered in order to get you a fair settlement. Sometimes it's both and sometimes there is really no question about either but still a matter of what the value of the case is. In all cases, it's very helpful to have an attorney make sure that all of these things are properly argued for you and ultimately, that you are treated fairly.

Strategies That Insurance Companies Use To Deny Claims

The insurance company is looking for any number of defenses to try to either deny or lower the value of your case. Deny, delay and defend is their mantra. One common defense an insurance company will use is to say that you had a gap in treatment or a time period in which you weren't treating. Therefore, you must not have been hurt, they will say, or you weren't hurt because of the car wreck, something else caused you to be hurt, you were already hurt, etc.

Sometimes, insurance companies will claim that if you went to the emergency room but you didn't go back to the doctor for days or a week, therefore, you don't have any claim beyond your emergency room treatment. That is a ridiculous defense for them to bring up and it's not a defense that usually would be successful for them in trial but it is a defense that they try. So, you do want to be aware of the defenses and you want to make sure that you are doing the things you need to do to protect yourself by getting timely treatment. You shouldn't let too much time go by while you're hurting without having or touching base with your doctors and having appointments. This is not in order to build up a claim for damages, this is to make sure that you are physically OK.

Moreover, there are lots of other things besides gaps in treatment that insurance companies will use to try to lower the value of your case. That could be the amount of property damage. They could say that if there is not enough property damage, then you weren't injured. That's often a defense that they will throw up and you should be at least aware of. They will also bring up your past medical history if you had been hurt before or injured in the same body part.

That's actually a double-edged sword that can work to your advantage because it might be more likely for someone who has been hurt before to get reinjured. But it can work to your detriment if the insurance company successfully says that you are really hurting because of this past injury and not because of any new injury from a car wreck. All of these are good reasons to have an experienced auto accident attorney who can help navigate all these defenses in ways that are advantageous to you. The bottom line is that it is bad enough to get injured in a car wreck, you shouldn't have to go at the legal process on your own and risk getting re-victimized by the process.

DOES DELAY IN TREATMENT MEAN YOU DON'T HAVE A PERSONAL INJURY CLAIM?

It's a very common scenario where people don't realize they are hurt initially. Medically and scientifically, most doctors will admit that it's very common for people to have adrenaline flowing that protects a person's mind from perceiving pain for some number of minutes or hours or sometimes even days after an initial injury. It is not at all uncommon for pain symptoms to flare up hours or days after the wreck. That does not mean that you don't have a claim even though an insurance company may say that or may say that that lowers the value of your claim.

Kevin Ginsberg has represented numerous people who didn't have their treatment start for some days after the car wreck. A week or two may not damage your claim too much but the longer it takes you to seek your first medical treatment, the less likely an insurance company or a jury will award you fair damages. Waiting longer than a couple of weeks will make you fall in the timeframe in which it's highly unlikely that you'll ever get fair compensation. That said, there is no rule about that. A personal injury attorney is fighting for the truth to prevail and if the truth is that you were hurt, you deserve fair compensation. But you should be aware of the defenses that insurance companies will use to minimize your claim.

In addition to just "what it looks like" to an insurance company or a juror, if you delay getting medical treatment, the insurance company might have a defense of a "failure to mitigate your damages" by not seeking timely treatment. This means that if, had you sought medical treatment sooner, your injury could've been cleared up more quickly, the insurance company doesn't have to pay for damages caused by your failure to get timely treatment. So, you're not doing anything unethical to go get treatment right away. You're not building a case. You are doing what you need to do for your health and in doing that, you're also protecting your legal case.

Follow The Recommended Treatment And Do Not Miss The Doctor's Appointment

That's one of the most important things about your case. Medical records are the biggest, usually the most voluminous and sometimes the most important, pieces of evidence of your case. It's necessary to have documented medical records from your medical providers and other healthcare providers. Without it, you don't have a case. If you have records that say that the patient was noncompliant or was missing an appointment, that's not going to help you; it's only going to hurt you.

While a lawyer can take a lot of the stress and strain away from you and make sure that you get treated fairly, the injured party has to take some of the responsibility. The main part of that responsibility is making sure that you are being responsible for your medical appointments, keeping the appointments, being on time and following the doctor's orders in honest efforts to heal.

COMMON MISCONCEPTIONS ABOUT AUTO ACCIDENT CASES

One of the most common misconceptions people have is that if you get into a car wreck, insurance will just handle everything, that you don't have to worry

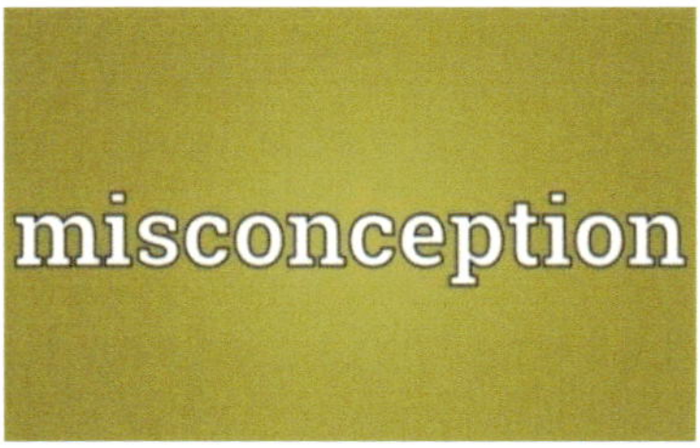

about it because there is insurance. Perhaps that is what should happen, but more often than not, you need a personal injury attorney to make sure that happens. People also assume, if you are in an accident, that you are automatically entitled to money. Although you should be entitled to fair compensation if you were injured and it was not your fault, getting in a car accident really does not entitle you to anything. There are certain facts and law that come into play that decide whether or not you have a legal case that allows for compensation.

People also have a misconception about the value of their case. While some areas of law, such as social security disability and workers' compensation, do have mathematical formulas involved in the computation of the value of claims, there has never been a formula in tort claims such as car wrecks; everything really is decided on a case by case basis. Back in the 1980s and 1990s, however, it was very common for people to get three times their medical bills. Again, that was never a rule or law, but it seems it did used to be easier for people to get fair compensation when injured. Unfortunately, those days are long gone because of tort reform and because of changes in the legal system and in the jury system culture. Every case is individual, and your attorney can advise you as to what the value of your case may be.

Another misconception people have is that if they don't have a perfect case, then they can't pursue it. You might have some difficult facts to deal with in your case but that does not mean that you don't have a valid case. Personal injury lawyers are used to dealing with hard facts. A good honest client with a good honest case should still get a good honest result even if there are some difficult facts to deal with.

Why Do You Need An Attorney In An Auto Accident Case?

As I said before, one of the most common misconceptions is that if you get into a car wreck, insurance will just handle everything. However, the reality is that insurance companies simply do not take unrepresented people seriously. There are certain adjusters whose job is to deal

with people who are not represented. When someone gets represented, your claim often goes to a different adjuster who handles represented claims, and the vast majority of the time, they are going to take your claim more seriously when an attorney is involved. They are going to give a better settlement where, even after the attorney's fee comes out, you're going to be much better off. Plus you will have the peace of mind of being able to focus on your own health and recovery rather than all the legal issues.

Any personal injury car wreck attorney who takes your case will do it on a contingency fee basis, which means that you will not have to write the attorney a check for his or her services. The attorneys' fee will be based on a percent of the settlement, so you and your attorney will be on the same side, both wanting the best result possible.

Like I said before, there is no way to put in writing something that would explain all the intricacies of your particular case. This is just an overview of a few of the big picture things to keep in mind. Your best protection is to consult with an attorney about your case, but hopefully this gives you a little bit of a sense of which direction to go. Good luck!

DISCLAIMER

This publication is intended to be informational only. No legal advice is being given, and no attorney-client relationship is intended to be created by reading this material. If you are facing legal issues, whether criminal or civil, seek professional legal counsel to get your questions answered.

Taibi Kornbluth Law Group, P.A.
3100 Tower Blvd., Suite 800
Durham, North Carolina, 27707
(919) 328-0508
www.personalinjurydurham.com

Made in the USA
Monee, IL
05 November 2026

67385073R00024